THE
W
HAM
UNITED
ANNUAL 2019

Written by Rob Pritchard
Designed by Adam Wilsher

g

A Grange Publication

© 2018. Published by Grange Communications Ltd., Edinburgh, under licence from West Ham United Football Club. Printed in the EU.

ISBN: 978-1-912595-22-8

CONTENTS

THIS ANNUAL BELONGS TO:

Jake

MY AGE:

7 3/4 8

MY SCHOOL:

Maldon Court

MY FOOTBALL TEAM:

Whitтом Town

MY POSITION:

all

MY FAVOURITE WEST HAM UNITED PLAYER:

Arnautovic

MY FAVOURITE FOOTBALL PLAYER:

Messi

**WHERE WEST HAM UNITED WILL
FINISH IN THE PREMIER LEAGUE:**

1st

MY 2018/19 PREMIER LEAGUE CHAMPIONS:

Juventus Barcelona West ham

MY 2019 FA CUP WINNERS:

Argentina, portgacal,

MY 2019 EFL CUP WINNERS:

barnsley

MY 2019 UEFA CHAMPIONS LEAGUE WINNERS:

West ham

9 THINGS YOU PROBABLY DIDN'T KNOW ABOUT WEST HAM UNITED

1 West Ham United have played at Wembley Stadium 12 times in the Club's history, winning seven matches, drawing two and losing just three. Of those victories, three have come in FA Cup finals and a fourth in the 1965 European Cup Winners' Cup final.

2 West Ham United became the last team to win the FA Cup while playing outside the top division when they beat Arsenal in the final in 1980.

3 Billy Bonds was aged 41 years and 226 days when he made his final appearance against Southampton in April 1988 — the oldest player in West Ham United's history!

4 The Hammers' all-time leading Premier League goalscorer is Italian forward Paolo Di Canio, who netted 47 in 118 appearances between 1999 and 2003.

6 The Club's first-ever club captain was Scottish full-back Bob Stevenson, who led Thames Ironworks FC in the 1895/96 season.

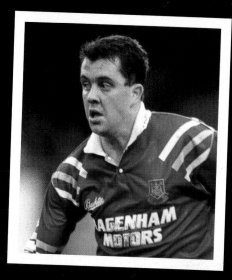

5 Four players whose surnames begin with the letter 'Z' have played for the Hammers — all of them since 2004 — Bobby Zamora, Mauro Zarate, Simone Zaza and Pablo Zabaleta!

7 West Ham have had nine different shirt sponsors since the first logo appeared in 1983 — AVCO Trust, BAC Windows, Dagenham Motors, Dr Martens, JobServe, XL Holidays, SBOBET, Alpari and, since February 2015, Betway.

8 The Hammers scored in 27 consecutive European matches between 1964 and 1980 — a record only beaten by Barcelona in 2011!

9 Brazil winger Felipe Anderson became the Club's record signing when he arrived from Italian side Lazio in July 2018.

2017/18
SEASON REVIEW

West Ham United secured their Premier League place with two games to spare at the end of a rollercoaster campaign

West Ham United kicked-off their second season at the London Stadium buoyed by the acquisition of several high-profile players.

Austrian attacker Marko Arnautovic arrived from Stoke and became the Club's record-signing, whilst prolific Mexican striker Chicharito returned to the Premier League after a stint in the Bundesliga at Bayer Leverkusen, as manager Slaven Bilic sought to bolster his team's attacking options.

Argentinian full-back Pablo Zabaleta and England goalkeeper Joe Hart, who both enjoyed trophy-laden spells at Manchester City, would bring their experience and pedigree to the squad.

AUGUST started with the squad missing several key players through injury including Manuel Lanzini and Michail Antonio, West Ham's

FIRST OF FOUR: Pablo Zabaleta was one of a quartet of experienced players to join West Ham United in summer 2017

Premier League campaign was to begin with a tough afternoon at Old Trafford. With Romelu Lukaku scoring twice, United inflicted a 4-0 defeat.

A week later, West Ham were unfortunate to come away from Southampton without a point after conceding an injury time penalty. The afternoon was marred by a red card for Arnautovic however two goals from Chicharito offered a perfect example of the Mexican's razor-sharp reactions in front of goal.

SEPTEMBER began with the Hammers' first home game, under the lights against Huddersfield. Two goals in the last twenty minutes from Pedro Obiang and Andre Ayew respectively sealed the win, giving Bilic the perfect present for his 49th birthday.

A goalless draw against West Brom followed before the visit of Bolton Wanderers in the Carabao Cup. Arthur Masuaku's 25-yard

MOST APPEARANCES
37
AARON CRESSWELL/
PABLO ZABALETA

MOST STARTS
36
AARON CRESSWELL

MOST MINUTES
3,186
PABLO ZABALETA

MOST GOALS
11
MARKO ARNAUTOVIC

MOST ASSISTS
7
AARON CRESSWELL

MATCHES	43
WINS	13
DRAWS	12
LOSSES	18

GOALS FOR
54
GOALS AGAINST
72
CLEAN SHEETS
13

strike was the pick of the goals as Bilic's side enjoyed a 3-0 win.

It was Arnautovic who would enjoy the praise of the manager the following game, after a performance which saw the Austrian set up two goals.

"He has got that quality and that something extra," said Bilic about the player whose importance to the team would grow as the season progressed.

A 3-2 defeat against rivals Tottenham Hotspur and a dramatic late win vs Swansea brought the month to a close.

After a two-week international break,

OCTOBER was to prove another frustrating month for the Hammers in the Premier League.

Draws against Burnley and Crystal Palace, with late equalisers conceded in both games, kept the Hammers in the bottom half of the table.

However, the unquestionable highlight of the first half of the season was a brilliant 3-2 Carabao Cup win against Spurs at Wembley.

West Ham looked dead and buried at half time, but buoyed by fantastic support from the Claret and Blue Army, completed a memorable comeback win with Angelo Ogbonna's superb 70th-minute header.

NOVEMBER heralded a change in management as the Club parted ways with Slaven Bilic and appointed former Manchester United and Everton manager David Moyes.

REVIEW CONTINUES OVERLEAF

NEW MAN IN CHARGE: David Moyes became West Ham United's 16th permanent manager in November

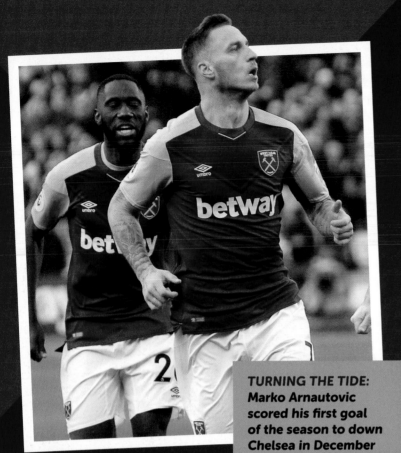

condemn West Brom to a 2-1 defeat.

Two days later, Pedro Obiang's brilliant 35-yard screamer against Tottenham at Wembley stunned the hosts, although the game ended in a draw.

The midfielder's amazing strike would go on to claim the Goal of the Season accolade at the Club's end-of-season Player Awards.

The January transfer window gave Moyes the opportunity to add to a squad that had suffered more than its fair share of injuries.

Portuguese playmaker Joao Mario arrived from Inter Milan in a loan deal, while young English striker Jordan

The new look coaching team, including former West Ham terrace-favourite and England full back Stuart Pearce, would bring experience and a fresh sense of impetus to a campaign that had begun disappointingly.

Moyes' reputation for organising defences and making his sides difficult to beat bore fruit in DECEMBER with a brilliant 1-0 win at home against Premier League champions Chelsea.

The Scot's deployment of Arnautovic in a central attacking role proved a masterstroke as the Austrian inspired a famous derby win. A goalless draw against Arsenal followed four days later and the Club went into the festive period with a renewed determination to climb the table.

A controversial late winner from Bournemouth striker Callum Wilson denied the Hammers a Boxing Day win on the South Coast as the game ended 3-3.

JANUARY's first fixture, saw a welcome return to the side of striker Andy Carroll who came off the bench to score twice and

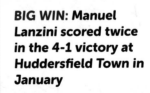

SEASON REVIEW

LANDMARK: Mark Noble scored his 50th goal for the Club against Crystal Palace in January

Hugill and veteran full-back Patrice Evra brought potential and pedigree respectively to the dressing room.

FEBRUARY's highlight was a 2-0 win against Watford at London Stadium before MARCH brought the opportunity to pick up more points and reach mid table.

After returning from a warm weather training camp in Miami a galvanised squad ensured that March ended with a hugely-important morale-boosting 3-0 win against Southampton, including brilliant goals from Arnautovic and Joao Mario.

Back-to-back draws in APRIL against Chelsea and Stoke brought Moyes' side tantalisingly-close to securing Premier League safety but it would not be until early MAY when Moyes' mission was accomplished.

A superb volley from skipper Mark Noble, wrapped up a 2-0 win at the 2015/16 champions Leicester, leaving the Claret and Blue Army to soak up the sunshine and look forward to another top-flight campaign, ahead of a season-ending 3-1 victory against Everton at London Stadium.

THINGS YOU MIGHT NOT KNOW ABOUT MANUEL PELLEGRINI

1 MANUEL PELLEGRINI IS FROM CHILE

The West Ham United manager was born in Santiago, the capital city of the South American country Chile, on 16 September 1953. How old does that make him?

2 HE WAS A ONE-CLUB MAN

Pellegrini the player was a tough-tackling centre-back who spent his entire 14-year career with the Universidad de Chile club, playing more than 500 times between 1973 and 1986. He did not win a single trophy, though!

3 HE HAS MANAGED 14 DIFFERENT CLUBS!

Pellegrini kicked-off his managerial career with Universidad de Chile in 1988 and, since then, has coached clubs in Chile, Ecuador, Argentina, Spain, England and China!

4 HE SIGNED CRISTIANO RONALDO

Pellegrini managed Real Madrid in 2009/10, signing Cristiano Ronaldo from Manchester United and leading a squad that also included Sergio Ramos, Pepe, Kaka, Xabi Alonso, Raul, Iker Casillas, Gonzalo Higuain and Karim Benzema!

5 HE WON THE PREMIER LEAGUE TITLE

Pellegrini guided Manchester City to the second Premier League title in the club's history in 2014, becoming the first non-European to manage the English champions.

6 HE IS A UNIVERSITY GRADUATE

Pellegrini has a degree in civil engineering from Universidad de Chile, earning him the nickname 'The Engineer'.

7 HE IS A UEFA CHAMPIONS LEAGUE REGULAR

Pellegrini has managed four clubs in the UEFA Champions League — Real Madrid, Manchester City, Villarreal and Malaga.

8 HE LOVES WINNING!

Before the 2018/19 season kicked-off, Pellegrini had taken charge of 603 matches in European football, winning 332 of them and losing just 156!

9 HE IS A HISTORY-MAKER

Pellegrini is the first South American to manage West Ham United.

- [ ] AFC BOURNEMOUTH
- [x] ARSENAL
- [ ] BRIGHTON AND HOVE ALBION
- [ ] BURNLEY
- [ ] CARDIFF CITY
- [ ] CHELSEA
- [ ] CRYSTAL PALACE
- [ ] EVERTON
- [ ] **FULHAM**
- [ ] HUDDERSFIELD TOWN
- [ ] LEICESTER CITY
- [ ] LIVERPOOL
- [ ] MANCHESTER CITY
- [ ] MANCHESTER UNITED
- [ ] **NEWCASTLE UNITED**
- [ ] SOUTHAMPTON
- [ ] TOTTENHAM HOTSPUR
- [ ] WATFORD
- [ ] **WEST HAM UNITED**
- [ ] WOLVERHAMPTON WANDERERS

TUNNELVISION

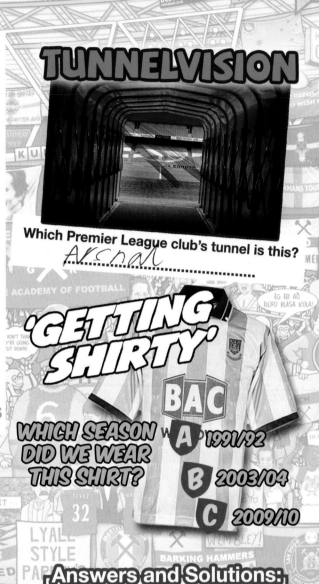

Which Premier League club's tunnel is this?

Arsenal

'GETTING SHIRTY'

WHICH SEASON DID WE WEAR THIS SHIRT?

A 1991/92

B 2003/04

C 2009/10

CAN YOU SPOT 5 DIFFERENCES BETWEEN THESE TWO PICTURES OF BOBBY MOORE SHAKING HANDS WITH THE PRESTON NORTH END CAPTAIN PRIOR TO THE 1964 FA CUP FINAL?

Answers and Solutions:

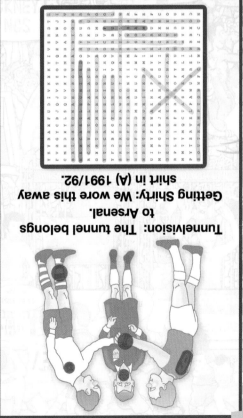

Tunnelvision: The tunnel belongs to Arsenal.

Getting Shirty: We wore this away shirt in (A) 1991/92.

GOALKEEPERS

The men whose job it is to keep the ball out of the West Ham United net

ADRIAN

Born: 3 January 1987, Seville, Spain
Appearances: 145
Clean Sheets: 41
Did you know: Adrian scored the decisive penalty in West Ham United's 9-8 FA Cup third-round shootout victory over Everton in January 2015.

JOSEPH ANANG

Born: 8 June 2000, Ghana
Appearances: 0
Clean Sheets: 0
Did you know: Joseph Anang trained with the Academy of Football throughout the 2017/18 season before being granted international clearance to play and signing his first pro contract in July 2018.

LUKASZ FABIANSKI

Born: 18 April 1985, Kostrzyn nad Odra, Poland
Appearances: 0
Clean Sheets: 0
Did you know: Lukasz Fabianski has travelled to four major tournaments with Poland — the 2006 and 2018 FIFA World Cup finals and UEFA Euro 2008 and 2016.

NATHAN TROTT

Born: 21 November 1998, Bermuda
Appearances: 0
Clean Sheets: 0
Did you know: Nathan Trott was an outfield player until the age of 15, when his coaches suggested his tall, athletic frame would be better suited to playing in goal!

*all stats correct up to July 2018

PHOTO QUIZ

Test your knowledge of West Ham United with our teasers!
Can you pick the correct answer from the three options?
Answers can be found on page 60-61!

1

Which Romanian international played 15 Premier League games for West Ham United during the 2013/14 season?
Razvan Rat
Ilie Dumitrescu
Florin Raducioiu

2

From which Spanish club did West Ham United sign goalkeeper Adrian in June 2013?
Racing Santander
Real Betis
Real Zaragoza

3

Who finished as West Ham United's leading assist-maker in the 2017/18 season?
Mark Noble
Aaron Cresswell
Manuel Lanzini

4

How many players made their West Ham United debuts at Liverpool on the opening day of the 2018/19 season?
Six
Seven
Eight

5

From which club did West Ham
United sign Marko Arnautovic?
Sunderland
Stoke City
Swansea City

6

Who captained West Ham United to
FA Cup glory in 1975 and 1980?
Bobby Moore
Billy Bonds
Trevor Brooking

7

Which South American country does
West Ham United manager Manuel
Pellegrini hail from?
Argentina
Brazil
Chile

8

Who scored West Ham United's
winning goal at Wembley in the
2012 Championship Play-Off final?
Ricardo Vaz Te
Carlton Cole
Kevin Nolan

9

Mark Noble is West Ham United's
all-time Premier League appearance
record holder, but who is second?
James Collins
Carlton Cole
Steve Potts

10

What squad number does Declan
Rice wear?
31
41
43

I'M FOREVER

WEST HAM UNITED LONDON

umbro

betway

2018/19 AWAY KIT AVAILABLE IN WEST HAM STORES AND ONLINE

OFFICIAL**WESTHAM**STORE.COM

STADIUM STORE
LONDON E20 2ST

BASILDON EASTGATE
BASILDON SS14 1EB

LIBERTY ROMFORD
ROMFORD RM1 3RL

LAKESIDE THURROCK
ESSEX RM20 2ZG

HERE COME THE GIRLS!

West Ham United women's team are competing in the FA Women's Super League for the first time this season

WEST Ham United women's team are midway through a historic season for the Club. Not only are the Hammers playing full-time professional football for the first time, but they are doing it as members of the FA Women's Super League — the highest tier of football for women in England. Then known as West Ham Ladies, the Club was accepted into the newly restructured FA WSL in June 2018, kicking-off an exciting and extremely busy summer.

CLAIRE RAFFERTY

ROSIE KMITA

ESMEE DE GRAAF

ANNA MOORHOUSE

BRIANNA VISALLI

BROOKE HENDRIX

LEANNE KIERNAN

Under the guidance of Managing Director Jack Sullivan and General Manager Karen Ray, the Hammers appointed a new coach with title-winning credentials in Matt Beard, a new backroom staff and set about assembling a new squad of top-class players.

First, 2017/18 captain Rosie Kmita was offered professional terms; the first female player in West Ham United history to be bestowed that honour.

Kmita accepted and she was not sat alone in the West Ham dressing room for long!

England defenders Claire Rafferty and Gilly Flaherty, along with goalkeeper Becky Spencer, joined from Chelsea, while Arsenal's Vyan Sampson and Anna Moorehouse, Americans Brooke Hendrix and Brianna Visalli, Scotland striker Jane Ross, Republic of Ireland forward Leanne Kiernan, Dutch trio, Tessel Middag, Esmee De Graaf and Lucienne Reichardt and Germany midfielder Julia Simic all followed them to east London.

When New Zealand international Ria Percival, exciting Swiss forward Alisha Lehmann and Liverpool midfielder Kate Longhurst also joined the Claret and Blue party, West Ham were ready to tackle their first campaign as professionals.

Based at Rush Green Stadium on the same site as the men's first team, the Hammers competed in the FA WSL, FA Women's Cup and FA WSL Continental Cup in 2018/19.

Head to whufc.com to find out more about this very special group of female footballers.

VYAN SAMPSON

JANE ROSS

JULIA SIMIC

KAREN RAY AND MATT BEARD WELCOME GILLY FLAHERTY

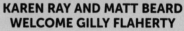

25

RECORD BREAKERS

YOUNGEST DEBUTANT
REECE OXFORD – 16 YEARS 198 DAYS V FC LUSITANOS (H), UEFA EUROPA LEAGUE FIRST QUALIFYING ROUND FIRST LEG, 2 JULY 2015

BIGGEST PREMIER LEAGUE WIN
6-0 V BARNSLEY (H), 10 JANUARY 1998

MOST APPEARANCES
799 – BILLY BONDS (1967-88)

MOST HAMMER OF THE YEAR AWARDS
5 – TREVOR BROOKING

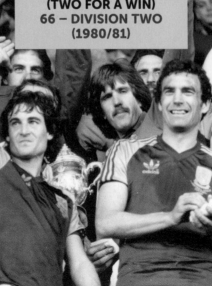

MOST POINTS IN A SEASON (TWO FOR A WIN)
66 – DIVISION TWO (1980/81)

OLDEST PLAYER
BILLY BONDS – 41 YEARS 226 DAYS V SOUTHAMPTON (A), FIRST DIVISION, 30 APRIL 1988

MOST POINTS IN A SEASON (THREE FOR A WIN)
88 – DIVISION ONE (1992/93)

MOST CLEAN SHEETS
146 – PHIL PARKES
(1979-90)

BIGGEST WIN
10-0 V BURY (H),
FOOTBALL LEAGUE CUP
SECOND ROUND SECOND
LEG, 25 OCTOBER 1983

**MOST PREMIER LEAGUE
APPEARANCES**
318 – MARK NOBLE
(2005-PRESENT)

HIGHEST ATTENDANCE
56,996 V MANCHESTER
UNITED, PREMIER
LEAGUE, 2 JANUARY 2017

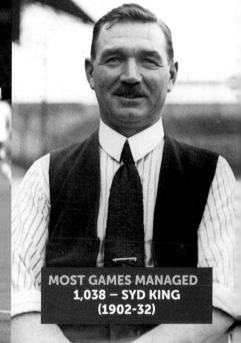

MOST GAMES MANAGED
1,038 – SYD KING
(1902-32)

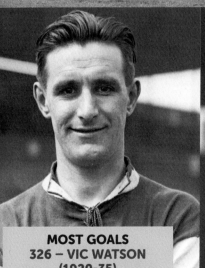

MOST GOALS
326 – VIC WATSON
(1920-35)

**MOST PREMIER LEAGUE
GOALS**
47 – PAOLO DI CANIO
(1999-2003)

DEFENDERS

The men who stand in the way of the opposition

PABLO ZABALETA

Born: 16 January 1985, Buenos Aires, Argentina
Appearances: 39
Goals: 0
Did you know: Pablo Zabaleta started all seven games for Argentina at the 2014 FIFA World Cup finals, including his country's 1-0 defeat by Germany in the final.

AARON CRESSWELL

Born: 15 December 1989, Liverpool, England
Appearances: 157
Goals: 5
Did you know: Aaron Cresswell became West Ham United's 40th England international when he debuted in a friendly against Spain at Wembley on 15 November 2016.

RYAN FREDERICKS

Born: 10 October 1992, Hammersmith, London, England
Appearances: 0
Goals: 0
Did you know: Ryan Fredericks was voted into the 2017/18 Championship PFA Team of the Year at right-back by his fellow professionals.

ANGELO OGBONNA

Born: 23 May 1988, Cassino, Italy
Appearances: 99
Goals: 4
Did you know: Angelo Ogbonna played for both Torino and Juventus in the Derby della Mole, the local derby contested by the two main clubs in the Italian city of Turin.

*all stats correct up to July 2018

29

DEFENDERS

The men who stand in the way of the opposition

WINSTON REID

Born: 3 July 1988, North Shore, Auckland, New Zealand
Appearances: 222
Goals: 10
Did you know: Winston Reid earned New Zealand their first-ever FIFA World Cup finals point when he headed the All Whites' last-minute Group F equaliser against Slovakia at South Africa 2010.

ARTHUR MASUAKU

Born: 7 November 1993, Lille, France
Appearances: 48
Goals: 1
Did you know: Arthur Masuaku won back-to-back Superleague Greece titles and one Greek Cup during a two-season stay with Olympiacos between 2014-16.

DECLAN RICE

Born: 14 January 1999, London, England
Appearances: 32
Goals: 0
Did you know: Declan Rice was aged just 19 years and 68 days when he made his senior Republic of Ireland debut in a friendly international in Turkey on 23 March 2018.

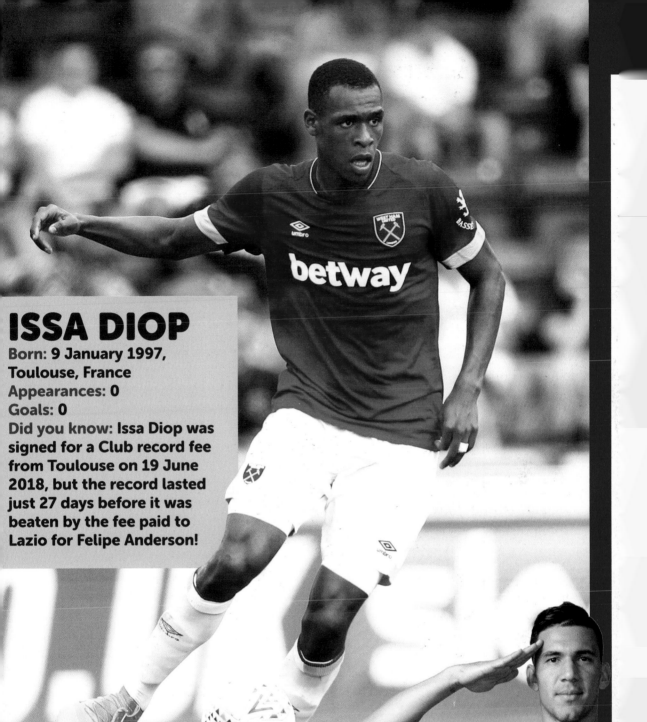

ISSA DIOP

Born: 9 January 1997, Toulouse, France
Appearances: 0
Goals: 0
Did you know: Issa Diop was signed for a Club record fee from Toulouse on 19 June 2018, but the record lasted just 27 days before it was beaten by the fee paid to Lazio for Felipe Anderson!

FABIAN BALBUENA

Born: 23 August 1991, Ciudad del Este, Paraguay
Appearances: 0
Goals: 0
Did you know: Fabian Balbuena's commanding defensive performances saw him earn the nickname el Comandante in Spanish, or O General in Portuguese, which both translate to The General in English.

*all stats correct up to July 2018

EAT LIKE A FOOTBALLER!

Follow a healthy, balanced lifestyle by eating the same meals as your Hammers heroes

EATING a balanced and nutritional diet is vital if footballers want to reach their maximum level of performance in every training session and match.

To do so, West Ham United players are provided with a diet that contains simple and complex carbohydrates, protein, fibre, vitamins, minerals and even some beneficial saturated and unsaturated fats.

Aside from three balanced main meals each day, footballers also benefit from snacking shortly after exercising, refuelling tired muscles.

At the same time, the players need to remain hydrated by drinking plenty of water and other drinks prescribed to them by the medical department, including taking on regular small quantities of liquid during training sessions and matches.

To help you to get started, here are three healthy dishes that you can try making with the help of an adult.

Remember to always wash your hands thoroughly with soap and warm water before handling raw food!

TERIYAKI SALMON

Fish is a staple part of many players' diets as it provides them with the proteins required to help the muscles to recover after a training session or match.

Teriyaki salmon is one of the most popular fish dishes we prepare, as it is both healthy and very tasty.

CHICKEN KORMA

Chicken Korma is a dish which ticks a number of boxes when it comes to fulfilling the players' nutritional requirements. The chicken itself contains protein, while the rice it is served with is a complex carbohydrate that contains minerals, vitamins and fibre.

STUFFED ROASTED BUTTERNUT SQUASH

Not every dish prepared for the players contains meat or fish, with vegetarian meals providing more of the complex carbohydrates which are used by the body to rebuild the sugar levels — glycogen stores — within the body at a faster rate.

WHAT TO EAT

If you are a footballer, it is important to eat a range of the following foods to provide the essential nutrients required to play your best in every training session and match:

Meat and meat alternatives — meat, fish, eggs, beans and nuts

Vegetables and fruit — root and leafy vegetables, salads, apples, oranges, bananas

Dairy products — milk, cheese, yoghurt

Starchy foods — bread, pasta, rice, cereals, potatoes

NEXT BIG THINGS

★ ★ ★ ★ ★ ★ ★ ★ ★ ★

Five Academy of Football stars to look out for in the future

AJIBOLA ALESE
DEFENDER
BORN: 17 JANUARY 2001

Not 18 until January 2019, centre-back Ajibola Alese's undoubted promise was rewarded with the signing of a first professional contract in July 2018.

Tall and strong, Alese has also developed the technical side of the game since joining West Ham United at the age of seven.

The 2017/18 season saw Alese represent the Hammers' U23s in Premier League 2 and England U17s at the UEFA European Championship finals.

MASON BARRETT
DEFENDER
BORN: 24 SEPTEMBER 1999

Injury may have slowed Mason Barrett's progress during the 2017/18 season, but the teenage defender has since returned to fitness and form and is eager to take the next step in his Claret and Blue career.

The centre-back's comeback from injury in February 2018 coincided with a marked upturn in form for West Ham's U18s, who won six of the nine games in which he featured last term.

A versatile player, Barrett is also capable of playing at right-back or in a defensive midfield role.

CONOR COVENTRY

MIDFIELDER

BORN: 25 MARCH 2000

The 2018 Dylan Tombides Award winner was a Republic of Ireland U19 international central midfielder named Conor Coventry.

A West Ham United player since the age of ten, Coventry was rewarded for his consistently impressive performances with a first professional contract in May 2017.

Since then, he has continued to progress, joining Manuel Pellegrini's first-team squad on their pre-season tour to Switzerland in July 2018.

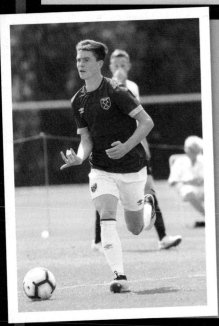

ALFIE LEWIS

MIDFIELDER

BORN: 28 SEPTEMBER 1999

A central midfielder in the Mark Noble mould, West Ham supporters were genuinely excited by Alfie Lewis's display in the first team friendly at Dagenham & Redbridge in spring 2018.

A confident ball player who is capable of opening the tightest of opposition defences, Lewis signed his first professional contract in May 2017 before making 15 appearances in Claret and Blue in 2017/18, including seven in Premier League 2 Division 1.

BERNARDO ROSA

FORWARD

BORN: 20 SEPTEMBER 2000

Born in Brazil and raised in England, Bernardo Rosa has taken the best ingredients from both countries to become a rounded attacking midfielder or forward.

Tall and confident with the ball at his feet, Rosa has played more than 30 times for the Hammers since breaking into the U18s during the 2016/17 season.

After featuring four times for the U23s in Premier League 2 in 2017/18, Rosa kicked-off the current season with a hat-trick for the U18s.

SPOT THE DIFFERENCE

Can you spot the ten differences between these two images of West Ham United's pre-season fixture at Preston North End? The answers can be found on pages 60-61!

WORDSEARCH

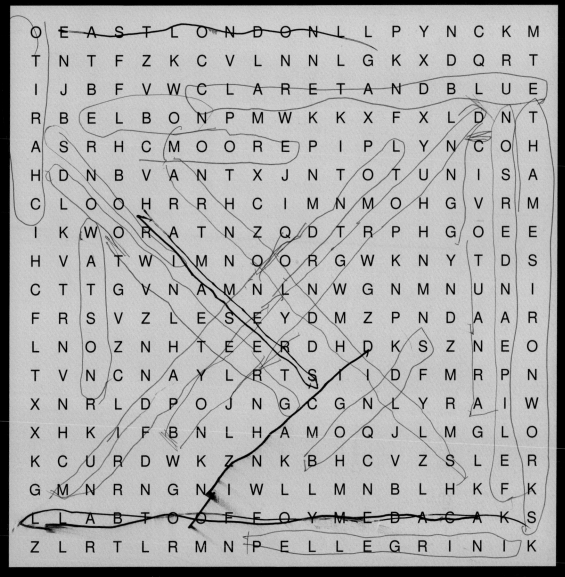

```
O E A S T L O N D O N I L L P Y N C K M
T N T F Z K C V L N N L G K X D Q R T
I J B F V W C L A R E T A N D B L U E
R B E L B O N P M W K K X F X L D N T
A S R H C M O O R E P I P L Y N C O H
H D N B V A N T X J N T O T U N I S A
C L O O H R R H C I M N M O H G V R M
I K W O R A T N Z Q D T R P H G O E E
H V A T W I M N O O R G W K N Y T D S
C T T G V N A M N L N W G N M N U N I
F R S V Z L E S E Y D M Z P N D A A R
L N O Z N H T E E R D H D K S Z N E O
T V N C N A Y L R T S I D F M R P N
X N R L D P O J N G C G N L Y R A I W
X H K I F B N L H A M O Q J L M G L O
K C U R D W K Z N K B H C V Z S L E R
G M N R N G N I W L L M N B L H K F K
L L A B T O O F F O Y M E D A C A K S
Z L R T L R M N P E L L E G R I N I K
```

Can you find the following West Ham United words and phrases in the wordsearch?
Answers can be found on page 60-61!

Arnautovic	Greenwood	Arnold Hills
Lanzini	Thames Ironworks	Di Canio
Claret and Blue	Chicharito	Irons
Hammers	Academy of	Felipe Anderson
Watson	Football	Bonds
London Stadium	Boleyn Ground	Pellegrini
Noble	Moore	East London

WEST HAM UNITED
LONDON

AUTOGRAPH:

MARKO
ARNAUTOVIĆ

A-Z OF WEST HAM UNITED

A is for **ALAN SEALEY**, the man who scored both goals in West Ham United's European Cup Winners' Cup final win over TSV 1860 Munich in 1965.

D is for **DI CANIO**, the Italian forward who remains West Ham's record Premier League scorer with 48 goals.

B is for **BILLY BONDS**, West Ham's all-time leading appearance maker with 799 between 1967-88.

E is for **ERNIE GREGORY**, who played in goal for 22 seasons and then coached for 27 more between 1938 and 1987.

C is for **CARLTON COLE**, the popular centre forward who made more substitute appearances for the Club, 111, than any other player.

F is for **FA CUPS**, which West Ham lifted in 1964, 1975 and 1980.

G is for **GREENWOOD**, the manager who led West Ham to their first major trophies in the 1960s.

L is for **LONDON STADIUM**, the 57,000-capacity venue which West Ham moved into in 2016.

O is for **OLYMPIC STADIUM**, which was converted into West Ham's London Stadium home following the 2012 London Games.

H is for **HMS WARRIOR**, the first ironclad warship in the Royal Navy, which was built by Thames Ironworks & Shipbuilding Company.

I is for **I'M FOREVER BLOWING BUBBLES**, the anthem sung by West Ham supporters since the 1920s.

M is for **MIKLOSKO**, the Czech goalkeeper who became the first overseas player to be crowned Hammer of the Year.

P is for **PAYET**, the only West Ham player to be nominated for the Balon D'Or while playing in Claret and Blue.

J is for **JOHN LYALL**, who played for, coached and managed the Club, winning the FA Cup in 1975 and 1980.

N is for **NOBLE**, the two-time Hammer of the Year, lifelong fan and all-time Premier League appearance record holder.

Q is for **HM The QUEEN**, who visited the Boleyn Ground to open the new West Stand in 2001.

K is for **KNIGHTS OF THE REALM** associated with the Club, Sir Trevor Brooking and Sir Geoff Hurst.

R is for **RIVET HAMMERS**, the tools used by shipbuilders which feature on West Ham's Club crest.

SCANDINAVIAN HAMMERS

S is for **SCANDINAVIAN HAMMERS**, West Ham's largest supporters' club, covering Denmark, Norway, Sweden, Finland and the Faroe Islands!

V is for **VAZ TE**, the man whose late goal fired West Ham to victory over Blackpool in the 2012 Championship Play-Off final.

X is for **XAVI VALERO**, West Ham's Spanish goalkeeper coach.

T is for **THAMES IRONWORKS FC**, the forerunner to West Ham United which existed between 1895 and 1900.

W is for **WATSON**, West Ham's all-time leading scorer with 326 goals.

Y is for **YOSSI BENAYOUN**, the Israeli playmaker who excited Hammers fans during two spells in the 2000s.

U is for **UPTON PARK**, the area of London in which West Ham played home games at the Boleyn Ground between 1904 and 2016.

Z is for **ZAMORA**, whose Play-Off final goal against Preston North End won promotion for the Hammers in 2005.

SOCIAL HAMMERS

Follow your favourite West Ham United players on social media!

	TWITTER	INSTAGRAM
ADRIAN	@AdriSanMiguel	adr13nsanmiguel
FELIPE ANDERSON	@F_Andersoon	f_andersoon
MARKO ARNAUTOVIC		m.arnautovic7
FABIAN BALBUENA	@FBalbuenito	fbalbuenito
ANDY CARROLL	@AndyTCarroll	andytcarroll
CHICHARITO	@CH14_	ch14
AARON CRESSWELL	@Aaron_Cresswell	cresser3
JOSH CULLEN	@JoshCullen	josh.cullen
ISSA DIOP		issa_diop_05
LUKASZ FABIANSKI	@lukaszfabianski	lukaszfabianski
RYAN FREDERICKS	@RyanFredericks_	
CHEIKHOU KOUYATE	@PapiCheikhou	roilionpapis8
MANUEL LANZINI	@manulanzini	manulanzini
ARTHUR MASUAKU	@arthurmasuaku	masuaku26
MARK NOBLE	@Noble16Mark	
PEDRO OBIANG	@obiang14	Pedrombaobiang
ANGELO OGBONNA	@OgbonnaOfficial	angeloogbonna21
MANUEL PELLEGRINI	@Ing_Pellegrini	
LUCAS PEREZ	@LP10oficial	10lp
WINSTON REID	@WinstonReid2	winston.reid2
DECLAN RICE	@_declanrice	_deccers10
CARLOS SANCHEZ	@carlossanchez6	carlossanchez6
ROBERT SNODGRASS	@robsnodgrass7	snods_10
JACK WILSHERE	@JackWilshere	jackwilshere
ANDRIY YARMOLENKO	@yarmolenko_9	yarmolenkoandrey
PABLO ZABALETA	@pablo_zabaleta	

MIDFIELDERS

The players who man West Ham United's engine room

MANUEL LANZINI

Born: 15 February 1993, Ituzaingó, Argentina
Appearances: 99
Goals: 20
Did you know: Manuel Lanzini has scored nine of his 20 goals for West Ham United in London derbies — four against Crystal Palace, three against Tottenham Hotspur and two against Chelsea.

ROBERT SNODGRASS

Born: 7 September 1987, Glasgow, Scotland
Appearances: 15
Goals: 0
Did you know: Robert Snodgrass became just the second Scotland player since 1969 to score a hat-trick when he netted three in a FIFA World Cup qualifier in Malta in September 2016.

PEDRO OBIANG

Born: 27 March 1992, Alcalá de Henares, Spain
Appearances: 87
Goals: 3
Did you know: Pedro Obiang scored his first goal for the Club on his 55th appearance in Claret and Blue in a Premier League win at Southampton on 4 February 2017.

JACK WILSHERE

Born: 1 January 1992, Stevenage, England
Appearances: 0
Goals: 0
Did you know: Jack Wilshere grew up in a family of West Ham United supporters and names Paolo Di Canio and Joe Cole as the players he idolised as a boy.

CARLOS SANCHEZ

Born: 6 February 1986, Quibdo, Colombia
Appearances: 0
Goals: 0
Did you know: Carlos Sanchez has featured for Colombia at two FIFA World Cup finals and three Copa America tournaments.

*all stats correct up to July 2018

MIDFIELDERS

The players who man West Ham United's engine room

REECE OXFORD

Born: 16 December 1998, Edmonton, London, England
Appearances: 17
Goals: 0
Did you know: Reece Oxford became West Ham United's youngest-ever player when he featured against Lusitanos of Andorra in the UEFA Europa League in July 2015, aged just 16.

NATHAN HOLLAND

Born: 19 June 1998, Wythenshawe, England
Appearances: 1
Goals: 0
Did you know: Nathan Holland made his Hammers debut in an EFL Cup win over Bolton Wanderers at London Stadium in September 2017.

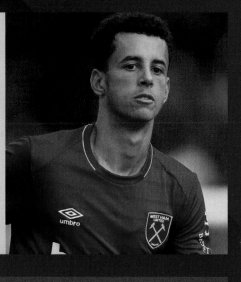

JOSH CULLEN

Born: 7 April 1996, Southend-on-Sea, England
Appearances: 9
Goals: 0
Did you know: Josh Cullen earned widespread respect when he continued playing in West Ham United's FA Cup third-round tie at Shrewsbury Town in January 2018, despite having one of his teeth kicked out!

MARCUS BROWNE

Born: 18 December 1997, London, England
Appearances: 1
Goals: 0
Did you know: Marcus Browne made his West Ham United debut in a UEFA Europa League play-off round tie at Romanian club Astra Giurgiu in August 2016.

MARK NOBLE

Born: 8 May 1987, Canning Town, London, England
Appearances: 435
Goals: 51
Did you know: Mark Noble made his 400th start for West Ham United in the 3-1 Premier League win over Everton at London Stadium on the final day of the 2017/18 season.

MOSES MAKASI

Born: 22 September 1995, London, England
Appearances: 0
Goals: 0
Did you know: Moses Makasi scored his maiden senior goal against Fleetwood Town during a loan spell with EFL League One club Plymouth Argyle in February 2018.

*all stats correct up to July 2018

MARKO ARNAUTOVIC
HAMMER OF THE YEAR!

Marko Arnautovic was crowned the 2017/18 Betway Hammer of the Year.

The Austria forward capped his outstanding debut season for West Ham United by becoming the 40th different player to win the acclaim of the Claret and Blue Army.

Arnautovic, who scored eleven goals and registered six assists, won 68 per cent of the vote, with Declan Rice finishing as runner-up, and Pablo Zabaleta third.

"This award that I have received, I am very happy and very proud," he said. "I want to keep doing my job for this Club because I came here to do my job and everybody has seen what I can do and that I'm very happy to be here and I want to keep doing it.

"I want to thank every single fan who supports West Ham for this award. It means a lot to me. It was hard for me at the beginning of the season but now it's going well and I want to do my job for many years to come. We are not finished yet.

"I try to do my best. All the players helped me. I love them and they love me!

"The best moment? Of course, scoring goals is a good moment for me, but to receive these awards is the best moment so far for me. I'll do my best in the last four games, I'll give everything and then we're going to go on holiday and come back and do better next season.

"Thank you all for this and I love you all!"

Arnautovic's Hammer of the Year award was one of three he took home from the 2017/18 Player Awards brought to you by Betway in aid of the Academy.

Among the other recipients on the night were Lifetime Achievement Award winner Ken Brown, who was the only Hammer to win the 1958 Second Division championship, the 1964 FA Cup and 1965 European Cup Winners' Cup, Pedro Obiang, Declan Rice, Conor Coventry and Ladies star Ellie Zoepfl.

2017/18 PLAYER AWARD WINNERS

**LIFETIME ACHIEVEMENT AWARD
KEN BROWN**

**LADIES PLAYERS' PLAYER OF THE YEAR
ELLIE ZOEPFL**

**GOAL OF THE SEASON
PEDRO OBIANG V TOTTENHAM**

**YOUNG PLAYER OF THE YEAR
DECLAN RICE**

**DYLAN TOMBIDES AWARD
CONOR COVENTRY**

WEST HAM UNITED LONDON

AUTOGRAPH:

MARK NOBLE

MATCH THE FACT TO THE HAMMER

Can you match the Hammer to the facts about their respective football careers? Answers can be found on page 61.

MARKO ARNAUTOVIC

JACK WILSHERE

DECLAN RICE

ADRIAN

MARK NOBLE

ANDRIY YARMOLENKO

PABLO ZABALETA

1 I made my England debut aged 18 years and 222 days against Hungary in August 2010

2 I started for my country in the 2014 FIFA World Cup final

3 I have played at the highest level in the Netherlands, Italy, Germany and England

4 I am West Ham United's all-time Premier League appearance record holder

5 I was released by Chelsea at the age of 13 but signed for West Ham United the following week!

6 I was voted my country's Footballer of the Year in 2013, 2014, 2015 and 2017

7 I take a yellow towel given to me by my family to every match I play in

7 THINGS YOU PROBABLY DIDN'T KNOW ABOUT LONDON STADIUM

Fascinating facts about West Ham United's home on Queen Elizabeth Olympic Park...

1 West Ham United's first-ever match at London Stadium was a UEFA Europa League qualifying round match against Slovenian side Domzale on 4 August 2016 — the Hammers won 3-0!

3 The London Stadium playing surface is a Desso GrassMaster artificial-natural hybrid pitch measuring 105 metres by 68 metres and is fitted with undersoil heating.

2 London Stadium has hosted a variety of events other than football, including the 2017 World Athletics and World Para Athletics Championships, the 2015 Rugby World Cup and concerts by the Rolling Stones, Jay-Z and Beyonce and Robbie Williams!

PLEASE KEEP OFF THE GRASS

4 London Stadium is on an island! the ground is surrounded by the River Lea, the City Mill River, Old Pudding Mill River, Bow Back Rivers and St Thomas' Creek.

7 The first hat-trick in London Stadium history was scored by Toni Martinez in an U23 Premier League win over Manchester United on 15 October 2017.

5 West Ham United's record attendance at London Stadium was the 56,996 who attended a Premier League fixture against Manchester United on 2 January 2017.

6 The stands behind the two goals were named in honour of Bobby Moore and Sir Trevor Brooking ahead of the Betway cup match with Juventus on 7 August 2016.

FORWARDS

The players charged with putting the ball in the net for West Ham United

MARKO ARNAUTOVIC

Born: 19 April 1989, Vienna, Austria
Appearances: 35
Goals: 11
Did you know: Marko Arnautovic has played in the top flight in the Netherlands, Italy, Germany and England, scoring more than 60 career goals.

ANDY CARROLL

Born: 6 January 1989, Gateshead, England
Appearances: 128
Goals: 33
Did you know: Andy Carroll scored the final hat-trick in Boleyn Ground history, in a 3-3 Premier League draw with Arsenal in April 2016.

CHICHARITO

Born: 1 June 1988, Guadalajara, Mexico
Appearances: 33
Goals: 8
Did you know: The son and grandson of Mexico internationals, Chicharito is his country's all-time leading scorer with 50 goals.

*all stats correct up to July 2018

FORWARDS

The players charged with putting the ball in the net for West Ham United

LUCAS PEREZ

Born: 10 September 1988, A Coruna, Spain

Appearances: 0

Goals: 0

Did you know: Lucas Perez was part of the Arsenal squad which won the FA Cup by defeating Chelsea at Wembley in May 2017.

TONI MARTINEZ

Born: 30 June 1997, Barrio del Progreso, Spain

Appearances: 3

Goals: 0

Did you know: Toni Martinez won promotion from the Spanish Segunda Division via the Play-Offs with Real Valladolid in June 2018.

ANDRIY YARMOLENKO

Born: 23 October 1989, St Petersburg, Soviet Union

Appearances: 0

Goals: 0

Did you know: Andriy Yarmolenko is the second-highest scorer in the Ukraine national team history behind all-time great Andriy Shevchenko and a four-time Ukrainian Footballer of the Year.

*all stats correct up to July 2018

DOWNLOAD THE OFFICIAL WEST HAM UNITED APP

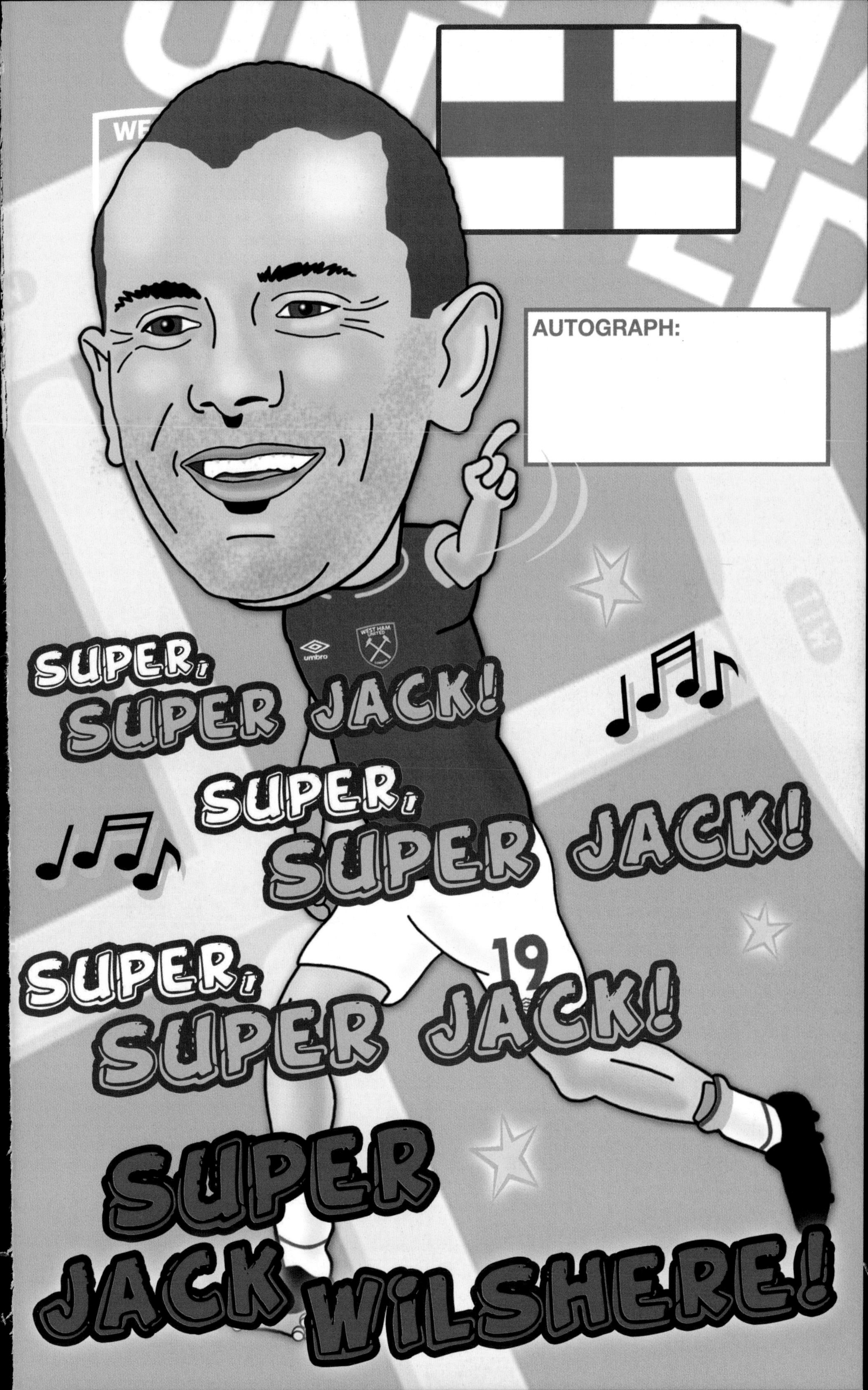

PUZZLE & QUIZ ANSWERS

PHOTO QUIZ PAGE 20-21

1. Razvan Rat, 2. Real Betis, 3. Aaron Cresswell, 4. six
5. Stoke City, 6. Billy Bonds, 7. Chile 8. Ricardo Vaz Te,
9. Carlton Cole, 10. 41

SPOT THE DIFFERENCE
PAGE 36

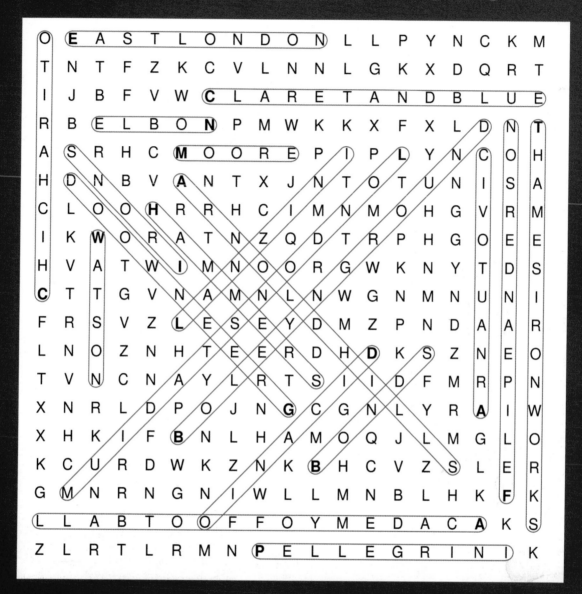

O E A S T L O N D O N L L P Y N C K M
T N T F Z K C V L N N L G K X D Q R T
I J B F V W C L A R E T A N D B L U E
R B E L B O N P M W K K X F X L D N T
A S R H C M O O R E P I P L Y N C O H
H D N B V A N T X J N T O T U N I S A
C L O O H R R H C I M N M O H G G R M
I K W O R A T N Z Q D T R P H G O E E
H V A T W I M N O O R G W K N Y T D S
C T T G V N A M N L N W G E M N U N I
F R S V Z L E S E Y D M Z P N D A A R
L N O Z N H T E E R D H D K S Z N E O
T V N C N A Y L R T S I I D F M R P N
X N R L D P O J N G C G N L Y R A I W
X H K I F B N L H A M O Q J L M G L O
K C U R D W K Z N K B H C V Z S L E R
G M N R N G N I W L L M N B L H K F S
L L A B T O O F F O Y M E D A C A K
Z L R T L R M N P E L L E G R I N I K

MATCH THE FACT TO THE
HAMMER PAGE 51

**1. Jack Wilshere, 2. Pablo Zabaleta, 3. Marko
Arnautovic, 4. Mark Noble, 5. Declan Rice,
6. Andriy Yarmolenko, 7. Adrian**